HA
BEARS

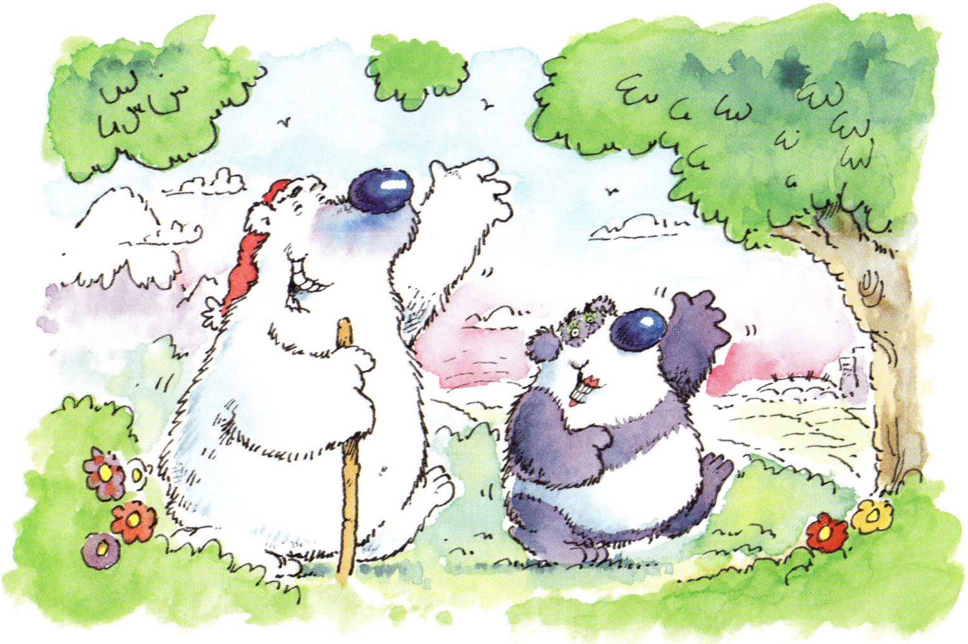

Written by Celia Warren
Illustrated by Mik Brown

Hairy bears from everywhere
went far away from home.

They set off for the fun fair
in the Big Bears' Dome.

Roly-poly polar bears
were wearing hairy white.
They slid across the ice
in the cold air of the night.

Hairy bears from everywhere
went far away from home.
They set off for the fun fair
in the Big Bears' Dome.

Big grumpy grizzly bears
were wearing hairy black.
No one dared to stop them.
They went tearing down the track.

Hairy bears from everywhere
went far away from home.
They set off for the fun fair
in the Big Bears' Dome.

Scary hairy mountain bears
were wearing coats of brown.
They made a careful landing
at the airport in the town.

Hairy bears from everywhere
went far away from home.
They set off for the fun fair
in the Big Bears' Dome.

A rare pair of pandas
with coats of black and white,
sailed across the ocean.
The bears were quite a sight!

Hairy bears from everywhere
went far away from home.
They set off for the fun fair
in the Big Bears' Dome.

One little teddy bear
made everybody stare.
He didn't have a hairy coat.
This teddy bear was bare!

"You're not a hairy bear.
You can't go in the Dome.
You can't go to the fun fair.
You must go back home."

"I'm a bear who is loved a lot.
My wear and tear shows it.
So I don't care if I'm bare
and everybody knows it."

Hairy bears from everywhere
hung their heads in shame.
"We've been unfair," they told the bear.
"We're very glad you came."

The hairy bears, to show they cared,
made him feel at home.
They all had fun at the fair
in the Big Bears' Dome.